Franklin Watts

First published in Great Britain in 2016 by The Watts Publishing Group

From the TV series *What's the Big Idea?* directed by Tanguy de Kermel,
© 2013 / 2014 Planet Nemo Animation / Skyline Entertainment / Motion Magic /
La Planète Rouge / Señalcolombia / Educar / Xilam Animation, loosely based
on the original work *Le livre des grands contraires philosophiques,* written by
Oscar Brenifier and illustrated by Jacques Després, pubished by Éditions Nathan.
Images taken from the Philozidées series, by the same authors from the same publisher.
Original script by Rachel Murrell.
First published in French as *Pourquoi je me mets en colère?*

Translation © Franklin Watts 2016
English text and adaptation by Elise Short

Series Editor: Elise Short
Series Advisor: Jackie Hamley
Design: Peter Scoulding and Cathryn Gilbert

Dewey number 152.4'7
HB ISBN 978 1 4451 4724 6

Printed in China

MIX
Paper from
responsible sources
FSC® C104740
FSC
www.fsc.org

Franklin Watts
An imprint of
Hachette Children's Group
Part of The Watts Publishing Group
Carmelite House
50 Victoria Embankment
London EC4Y 0DZ

An Hachette UK Company

www.hachette.co.uk

www.franklinwatts.co.uk

Why am I angry?

W
FRANKLIN WATTS
LONDON•SYDNEY

Hugo is very happy: he has just won a long and difficult game of draughts against his friend Yeti!

Yeti, however,
is very, very cross!
"Grooooaaarrr,"
he roars. He hates losing!

"Why are you cross, Yeti?" asks Hugo. "That was a fun game, wasn't it?"

Yeti just slams the door without even answering. He seems to be angry with Hugo for winning!

"That's unfair," thinks Hugo. "I didn't cheat!"

To celebrate his win, Hugo buys a vanilla ice cream from the ice cream girl.

"I never get angry. I always keep calm and smile!" he boasts.

He has not spotted the little monkey sneaking up on him...

Oh no! The monkey has snatched Hugo's ice cream!

"Heeeey!" yells Hugo. "Give me back my ice cream, you naughty monkey! Just wait till I catch you!"

So, keeping calm isn't that easy for Hugo after all – especially when someone steals his ice cream!

"Oh, Hugo, look at you!"
the ice cream girl says, handing
him a mirror.
Hugo has gone bright red. He's
frowning and clenching his teeth...
There's no hiding his anger: it's
written all over his face!

Meanwhile, Hugo's friend, Lucas, is feeling angry too. The llama just won't let him climb on its back!

"But it could be so much fun," Lucas sighs.

He has another go... but the llama jumps out of the way!

Ouch! Lucas lands on the floor!

Since he can't ride the llama, Lucas decides to jump into a racing car.

"At least the car will let me **do what I want**!"

Hugo is supposed to join him on the racetrack, but the monkey has got there first... and he can't drive for peanuts!

Whoopee! Lucas has won the race!

The monkey is furious at having lost, so he decides to steal Lucas's car to get even.

But Lucas won.

Should he be blamed for the monkey going bananas?

Moments later, the monkey **loses control** of the car and crashes into the stage at a concert.

Crash! Bang! The guitarist falls off the stage, the music stops... the concert is ruined!

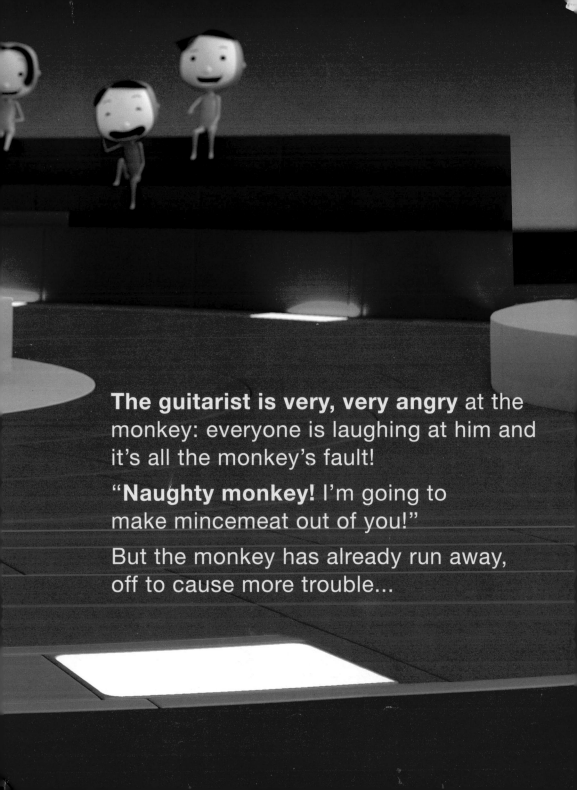

The guitarist is very, very angry at the monkey: everyone is laughing at him and it's all the monkey's fault!

"Naughty monkey! I'm going to make mincemeat out of you!"

But the monkey has already run away, off to cause more trouble...

Oh no, here he is! He's come to annoy Hugo and Yeti who are friends again.

Splash! And he's in the water! Yeti fishes him out by the tail.

The monkey is so funny that Hugo can't stay angry.

"Careful! Don't hurt him, Yeti!" he says.

Sometimes, we want something very badly but we can't have it...

Other times, we think something is really unfair, or we feel upset...

Then anger grows and grows and grows inside us! And we can't help but show the people around that we don't agree, that there's something making us really unhappy.

When the anger goes away, it's a good idea to calmly talk about it with the people who made us angry.

What do you think?

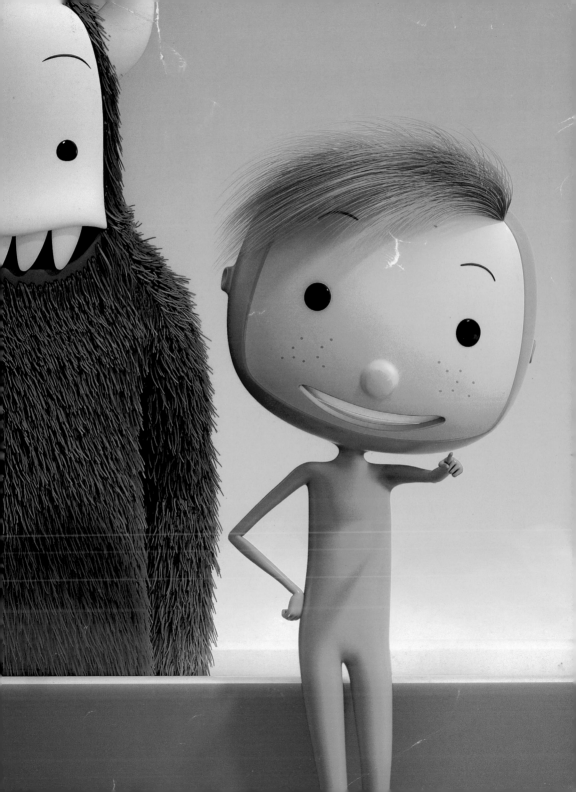

A note about sharing this book

The *What's the Big Idea?* series has been developed to provide a starting point for introducing philosophy to young children. It aims to promote thinking skills in its readers, developing their ability to ask questions about the world around them and encouraging them to make up their own mind about ideas and abstract concepts.

Why Am I Angry?

This story explores the effects of anger and the situations in which it arises. It also encourages children to think about what anger is and how to deal with it.

After reading, talk about the book with the children:

• What was the story about? Why did Yeti, Hugo, the monkey, etc. feel angry? What happened when they got angry? Have the children ever felt angry about someone or something? Encourage the children to draw on their own experiences.

• At the end of the story, it says that after we've stopped feeling angry, it's a good idea to calmly talk about what upset us with the people who made us angry. Why?

• Why do we get angry? Who do we get angry with? Are there different sorts of anger? Explain your answer with examples.

• Would it be good if nobody ever got angry? Is anger always bad? Explain your answers with examples.